Evaluation of the Sensitivity of Inventory and Monitoring National Parks to Nutrient Enrichment Effects from Atmospheric Nitrogen Deposition

Eastern Rivers and Mountains Network (ERMN)

Natural Resource Report NPS/NRPC/ARD/NRR—2011/307

T. J. Sullivan
T. C. McDonnell
G. T. McPherson
S. D. Mackey
D. Moore

E&S Environmental Chemistry, Inc.
P.O. Box 609
Corvallis, OR 97339

February 2011

U.S. Department of the Interior
National Park Service
Natural Resource Program Center
Denver, Colorado

The National Park Service, Natural Resource Program Center publishes a range of reports that address natural resource topics of interest and applicability to a broad audience in the National Park Service and others in natural resource management, including scientists, conservation and environmental constituencies, and the public.

The Natural Resource Report Series is used to disseminate high-priority, current natural resource management information with managerial application. The series targets a general, diverse audience, and may contain NPS policy considerations or address sensitive issues of management applicability.

All manuscripts in the series receive the appropriate level of peer review to ensure that the information is scientifically credible, technically accurate, appropriately written for the intended audience, and designed and published in a professional manner.

This report received peer review by subject-matter experts who were not directly involved in the collection, analysis, or reporting of the data. Data in this report were collected and analyzed using methods based on established, peer-reviewed protocols and were analyzed and interpreted within the guidelines of the protocols.

Views, statements, findings, conclusions, recommendations, and data in this report do not necessarily reflect views and policies of the National Park Service, U.S. Department of the Interior. Mention of trade names or commercial products does not constitute endorsement or recommendation for use by the U.S. Government.

This report is available from Air Resources Division of the NPS (http://www.nature.nps.gov/air/Permits/ARIS/networks/n-sensitivity.cfm) and the Natural Resource Publications Management website (http://www.nature.nps.gov/publications/nrpm/).

Please cite this publication as:

Sullivan, T. J., T. C. McDonnell, G. T. McPherson, S. D. Mackey, and D. Moore. 2011. Evaluation of the sensitivity of inventory and monitoring national parks to nutrient enrichment effects from atmospheric nitrogen deposition: Eastern Rivers and Mountains Network (ERMN). Natural Resource Report NPS/NRPC/ARD/NRR—2011/307. National Park Service, Denver, Colorado.

NPS 962/106647, February 2011

Eastern Rivers and Mountains Network (ERMN)

National maps of atmospheric N emissions and deposition are provided in Maps A and B as context for subsequent network data presentations. Map A shows county level emissions of total N for the year 2002. Map B shows total N deposition, again for the year 2002.

The Eastern Rivers and Mountains Network contains two parks that are slightly larger than 100 square miles: Delaware Water Gap (DEWA) and New River Gorge (NERI). In addition, there are seven smaller parks. Atmospheric N deposition is relatively high throughout much of the network.

Total N emissions, by county, are shown in Map C for lands in and surrounding the Eastern Rivers and Mountains Network. County-level annual emissions within the network ranged from less than 1 ton per square mile to greater than 100 tons per square mile. In general, county annual emissions were between 1 and 20 tons per square mile. A number of counties along the western border of the network showed total N annual emissions higher than 50 tons per square mile. Point source emissions of oxidized (nitrogen oxides, NO_x) and reduced (ammonia, NH_3) N are shown in Map D. The largest point sources were consistently sources of oxidized, rather than reduced, N. Many NO_x point sources in and around the network were larger than 5,000 tons per year, mainly located in the mid-section of the network. Urban centers within the network and within a 300-mile buffer around the network are shown in Map E. There are no population centers within the network (except Philadelphia, which is on the network border) that are larger than 500,000 people, but there are several in the range of 100,000 to 500,000 people.

Total N deposition in and around the network is shown in Map F. Included in this analysis are both wet and dry forms of N deposition and both the oxidized and reduced N species. Total N deposition within the network ranged from as low as 5 to 10 kg N/ha/yr to as high as 15 to 20 kg N/ha/yr. Almost the entire network receives in excess of 10 kg N/ha/yr of total N deposition.

Land cover in and around the network is shown in Map G. The predominant cover types within this network are generally forest, pasture/hay, developed areas, and row crops.

There are many parks within this network, but none are large enough to reveal spatial patterns in vegetation types at the scale of the network. Therefore, a map showing the presence of sensitive vegetation types (Map H) is not provided.

Park lands requiring special protection against potential adverse impacts associated with nutrient N enrichment from atmospheric N deposition are shown in Map I. Also shown on Map I are all federal lands designated as wilderness, both lands managed by NPS and also lands managed by other federal agencies. The land designations used to identify this heightened protection included Class I designation under the CAAA and wilderness designation. There are no Class I areas in this network and only limited designated wilderness, none of which is on lands managed by NPS.

Network rankings are given in Figures A through C as the average ranking of the Pollutant Exposure, Ecosystem Sensitivity, and Park Protection metrics, respectively. Figure D shows the overall network Summary Risk ranking. In each figure, the rank for this particular network is highlighted to show its relative position compared with the ranks of the other 31 networks.

The Eastern Rivers and Mountains Network ranks in the top quintile, one of the highest among the networks, in N Pollutant Exposure (Figure A). Nitrogen emissions and N deposition within the network are both Very High. However, the network Ecosystem Sensitivity ranking is Very Low, within the lowest quintile among networks (Figure B). This is because there are no high-elevation lakes, and there is limited coverage within this network of vegetation types that are among those expected to be especially sensitive to nutrient enrichment effects from N deposition. This network also ranks in the lowest quintile in Park Protection, having limited amounts of protected lands (Figure C).

In combination, the network rankings for Pollutant Exposure, Ecosystem Sensitivity, and Park Protection yield an overall Network Risk ranking that is in the lowest quintile, compared with other networks (Figure D). The overall level of concern for nutrient N enrichment effects on I&M parks within this network is considered Very Low.

Similarly, park rankings are given in Figures E through H for the same metrics. In the case of the park rankings, we only show in the figures the parks that are larger than 100 square miles. Relative ranks for all parks, including the smaller parks, are given in Table A and Appendix B. As for the network ranking figures, the park ranking figures highlight those parks that occur in this network to show their relative position compared with parks in the other 31 networks. Note that the rankings shown in Figures E through H reflect the rank of a given park compared with all other parks, irrespective of size.

The two I&M parks in the Eastern Rivers and Mountains Network that are larger than 100 square miles are ranked Very High (DEWA) and High (NERI) among parks in Pollutant Exposure (Figure E). Ecosystem Sensitivity rankings for these two parks are lower, with DEWA ranked Low and NERI ranked Very Low (Figure F). The smaller parks in this network are mostly ranked Low or Very Low in Ecosystem Sensitivity; two of the smaller parks (Fort Necessity, FONE; Johnstown Flood, JOFL) are ranked Moderate for this theme. Park Protection rankings for all parks in the network are Moderate (Table A, Figure G). The Summary Park Risk rankings for the two larger parks are High (DEWA) and Low (NERI) among all parks (Figure H). For the smaller parks in this network, the Summary Risk ranking is variable (Table A), from Very Low for Bluestone (BLUE) to High for Allegheny Portage Railroad (ALPO), FONE, Friendship Hill (FRHI), and JOFL.

Table A. Relative rankings of individual I&M parks within the network for Pollutant Exposure, Ecosystem Sensitivity, Park Protection, and Summary Risk from atmospheric nutrient N enrichment.

I&M Parks[2] in Network	Relative Ranking of Individual Parks[1]			
	Pollutant Exposure	Ecosystem Sensitivity	Park Protection	Summary Risk
Allegheny Portage Railroad	Very High	Low	Moderate	High
Bluestone	Moderate	Very Low	Moderate	Very Low
Delaware Water Gap	Very High	Low	Moderate	High
Fort Necessity	Very High	Moderate	Moderate	High
Friendship Hill	Very High	Low	Moderate	High
Gauley River	High	Very Low	Moderate	Low
Johnstown Flood	Very High	Moderate	Moderate	High
New River Gorge	High	Very Low	Moderate	Low
Upper Delaware	High	Very Low	Moderate	Moderate

[1] Relative park rankings are designated according to quintile ranking, among all I&M Parks, from the lowest quintile (very low risk) to the highest quintile (very high risk).

[2] Park name is printed in bold italic for parks larger than 100 square miles.

Map A.   National map of total N emissions by county for the year 2002. Both oxidized (nitrogen oxides, NO_x) and reduced (ammonia, NH_3) forms of N are included. The total is expressed in tons per square mile per year. (Source of data: EPA National Emissions Inventory, http://www.epa.gov/ttn/chief/net/2002inventory.html)

Map B.   Total N deposition for the conterminous United States for the year 2002, expressed in units of kilograms of N deposited from the atmosphere to the earth surface per hectare per year. Wet and dry forms of both oxidized (nitrogen oxides, NO_x) and reduced (ammonia, NH_3) N are included. For the eastern half of the country, wet deposition values were derived from interpolated measured values from NADP (three-year average centered on 2002) and dry deposition values were derived from 12-km CMAQ model projections for 2002. For the western half of the country, both wet and dry deposition values were derived from 36-km CMAQ model projections for 2002. NADP interpolations were performed using the approach of Grimm and Lynch (1997). CMAQ model projections were provided by Robin Dennis, U.S. EPA.

Map C.   Total N emissions by county for lands surrounding the network, expressed as tons of N emitted into the atmosphere per square mile per year. The total includes both oxidized (nitrogen oxides, NO_x) and reduced (ammonia, NH_3) N. (Source of data: EPA National Emissions Inventory, http://www.epa.gov/ttn/chief/net/2002inventory.html)

Map D.   Major point source emissions of oxidized (nitrogen oxides, NO_x) and reduced (ammonia, NH_3) N in and around the network. The base of each vertical bar is positioned in the map at the approximate location of the source. The height of the bar is proportional to the magnitude of the source. (Source of data: EPA National Emissions Inventory, http://www.epa.gov/ttn/chief/net/2002inventory.html)

Map E. Urban centers having more than 10,000 people within the network and within a 300-mile buffer around the perimeter of the network. (Source of data: U.S. Census 2000)

Map F. Total N deposition in and around the network. Included in the total are wet plus dry forms of both oxidized (nitrogen oxides, NO_x) and reduced (ammonia, NH_3) N. Values are expressed as kilograms of N deposited per hectare per year. (Source of data: Interpolated NADP wet and CMAQ Model dry deposition data for 2002; see information for Map B above for details)

Map G. Land cover types in and around the network, based on the National Land Cover dataset. (Source of data: National Land Cover Dataset, http://www.mrlc.gov/nlcd_multizone_map.php)

Map I. Lands within the network that are classified as Class I or wilderness area. (Source of data: USGS 2005 [National Atlas; http://nationalatlas.gov] and NPS)

Figure A. Network rankings for Pollutant Exposure, calculated as the average of scores for all Pollutant Exposure variables.

Figure B. Network rankings for Ecosystem Sensitivity, calculated as the average of scores for all Ecosystem Sensitivity variables.

Figure C. Network rankings for Park Protection, calculated as the average of scores for all Park Protection variables.

Figure D. Network Summary Risk ranking, calculated as the sum of the averages of the scores for Pollutant Exposure, Ecosystem Sensitivity, and Park Protection.

Figure E. Park rankings for Pollutant Exposure for all parks larger than 100 square miles. Ranks for each park were calculated relative to all parks, regardless of size, as the average of scores for all Pollutant Exposure variables.

Figure F. Park rankings for Ecosystem Sensitivity for all parks larger than 100 square miles. Ranks for each park were calculated relative to all parks, regardless of size, as the average of scores for all Ecosystem Sensitivity variables.

Figure G. Park rankings for Park Protection for all parks larger than 100 square miles. Ranks for each park were calculated relative to all parks, regardless of size, as the average of scores for all Park Protection variables.

Figure H. Park rankings for Summary Risk for all parks larger than 100 square miles. Ranks for each park were calculated relative to all parks, regardless of size, as the average of scores for all Summary Risk variables.

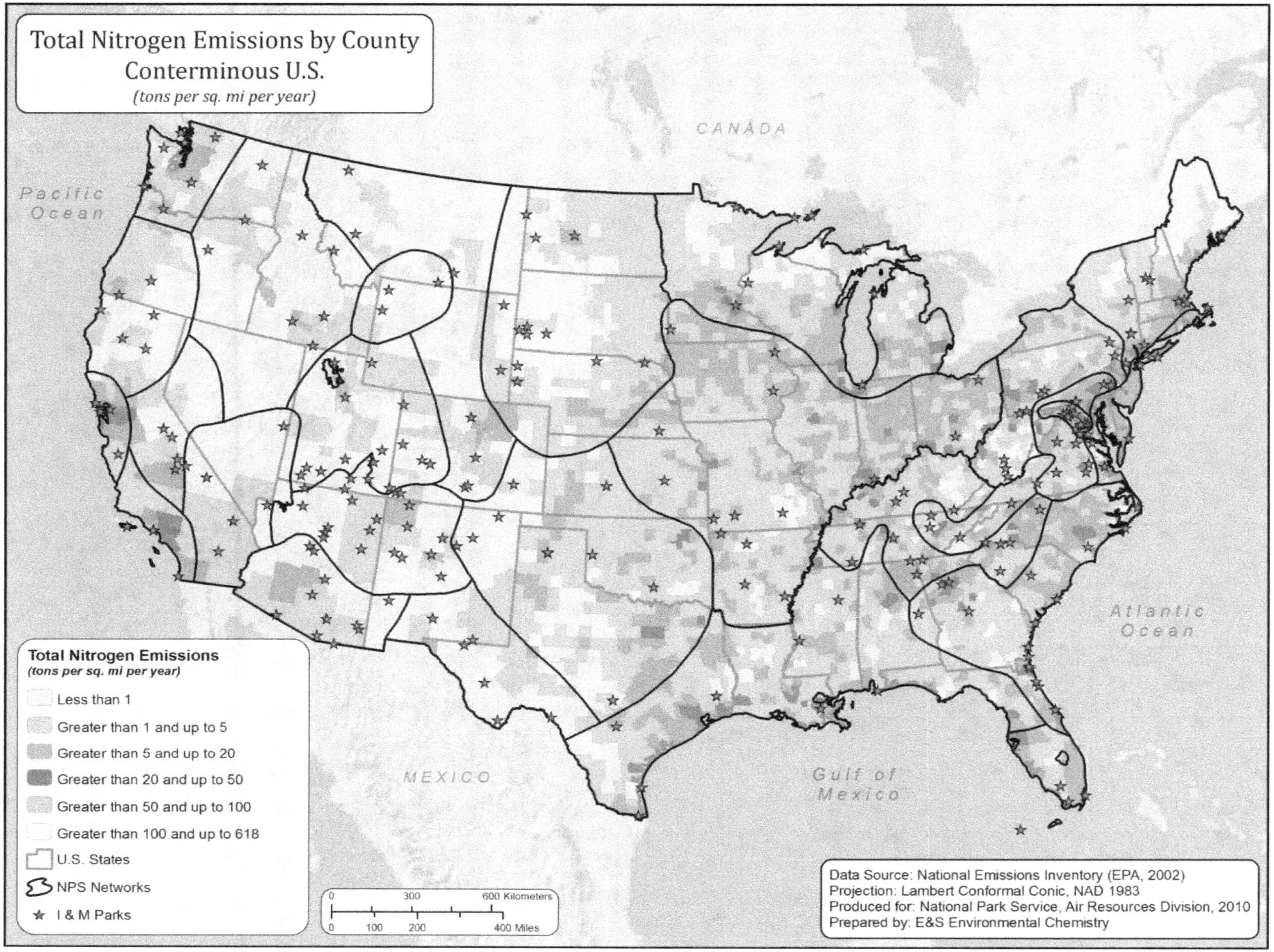

Total Nitrogen Emissions by County
Conterminous U.S.
(tons per sq. mi per year)
CANADA
Pacific Ocean
Atlantic Ocean
MEXICO
Gulf of Mexico
Total Nitrogen Emissions
(tons per sq. mi per year)
Less than 1
Greater than 1 and up to 5
Greater than 5 and up to 20
Greater than 20 and up to 50
Greater than 50 and up to 100
Greater than 100 and up to 618
U.S. States
NPS Networks
I & M Parks
0 300 600 Kilometers
0 100 200 400 Miles
Data Source: National Emissions Inventory (EPA, 2002)
Projection: Lambert Conformal Conic, NAD 1983
Produced for: National Park Service, Air Resources Division, 2010
Prepared by: E&S Environmental Chemistry

Map A

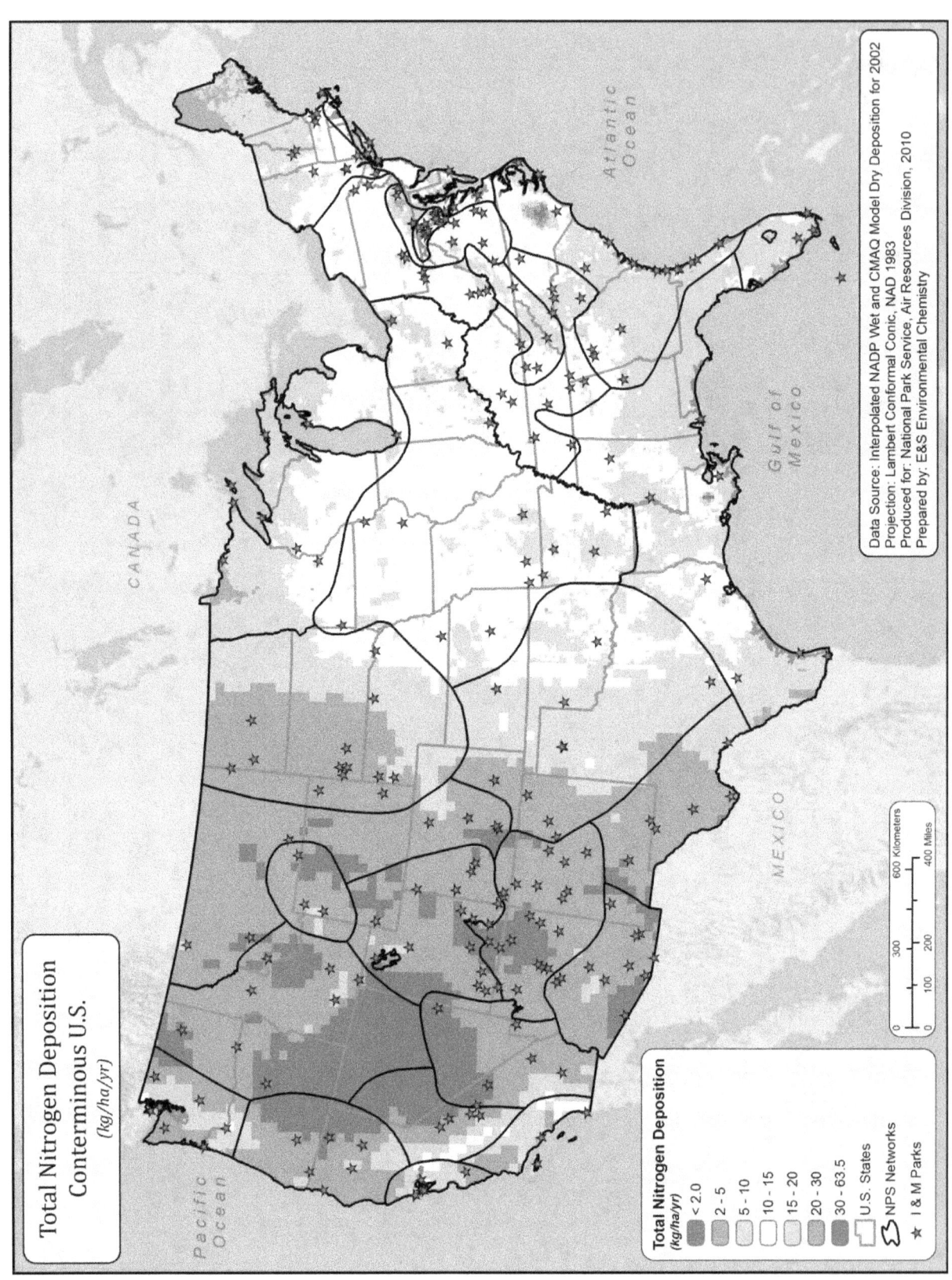

Total Nitrogen Deposition
Conterminous U.S.
(kg/ha/yr)

Total Nitrogen Deposition
(kg/ha/yr)
- < 2.0
- 2 - 5
- 5 - 10
- 10 - 15
- 15 - 20
- 20 - 30
- 30 - 63.5
- U.S. States
- NPS Networks
- I & M Parks

Data Source: Interpolated NADP Wet and CMAQ Model Dry Deposition for 2002
Projection: Lambert Conformal Conic, NAD 1983
Produced for: National Park Service, Air Resources Division, 2010
Prepared by: E&S Environmental Chemistry

Pacific Ocean

Atlantic Ocean

Gulf of Mexico

CANADA

MEXICO

0 100 200 300 600 Kilometers
0 200 400 Miles

Map B

CAKN-6

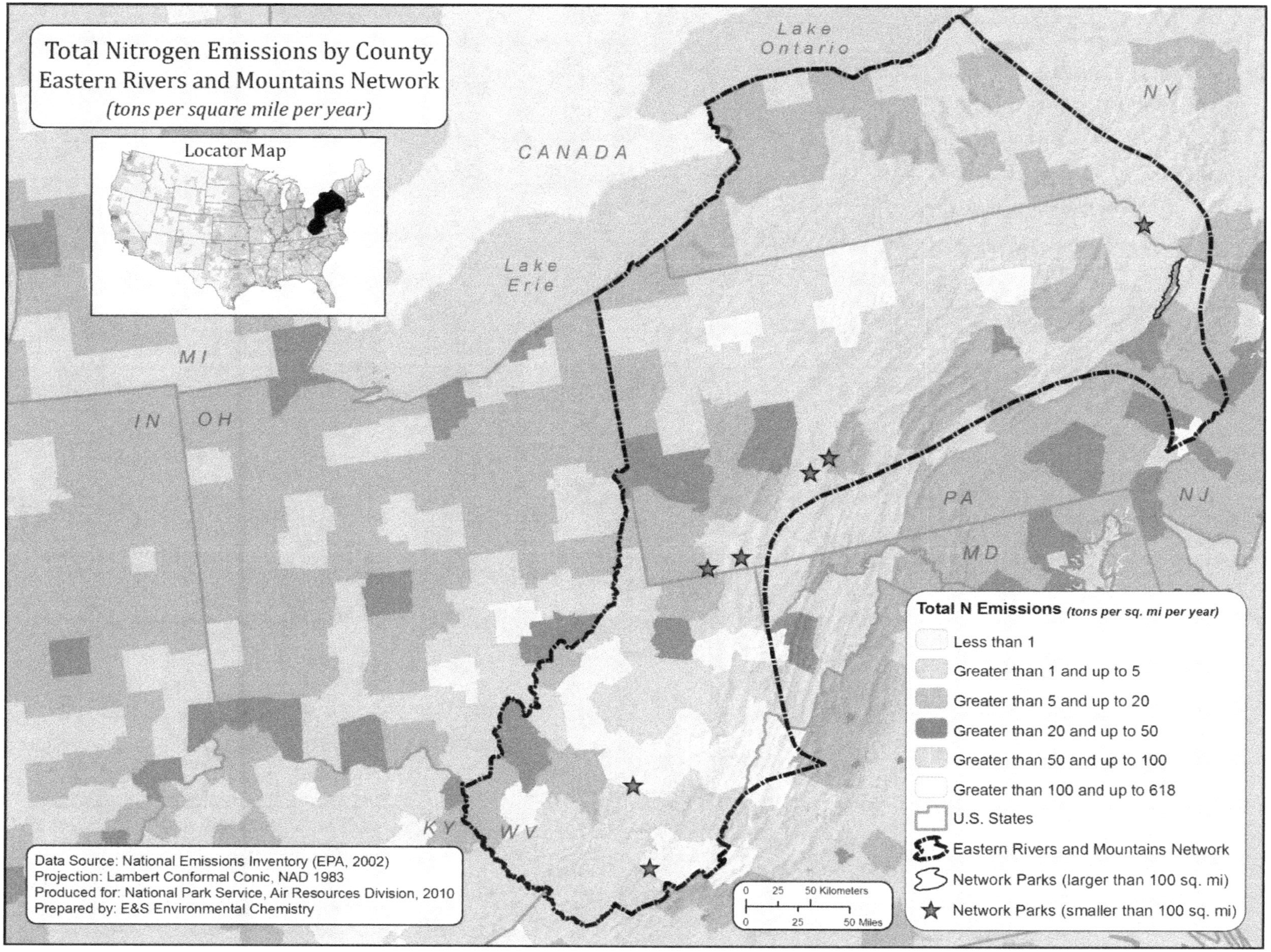

Total Nitrogen Emissions by County
Eastern Rivers and Mountains Network
(tons per square mile per year)

Locator Map

Total N Emissions *(tons per sq. mi per year)*

Less than 1
Greater than 1 and up to 5
Greater than 5 and up to 20
Greater than 20 and up to 50
Greater than 50 and up to 100
Greater than 100 and up to 618
U.S. States
Eastern Rivers and Mountains Network
Network Parks (larger than 100 sq. mi)
Network Parks (smaller than 100 sq. mi)

N Y

Lake Ontario

CANADA

Lake Erie

M I

I N

O H

P A

M D

N J

W V

K Y

Data Source: National Emissions Inventory (EPA, 2002)
Projection: Lambert Conformal Conic, NAD 1983
Produced for: National Park Service, Air Resources Division, 2010
Prepared by: E&S Environmental Chemistry

0   25   50 Kilometers
0   25   50 Miles

Map C

CAKN-7

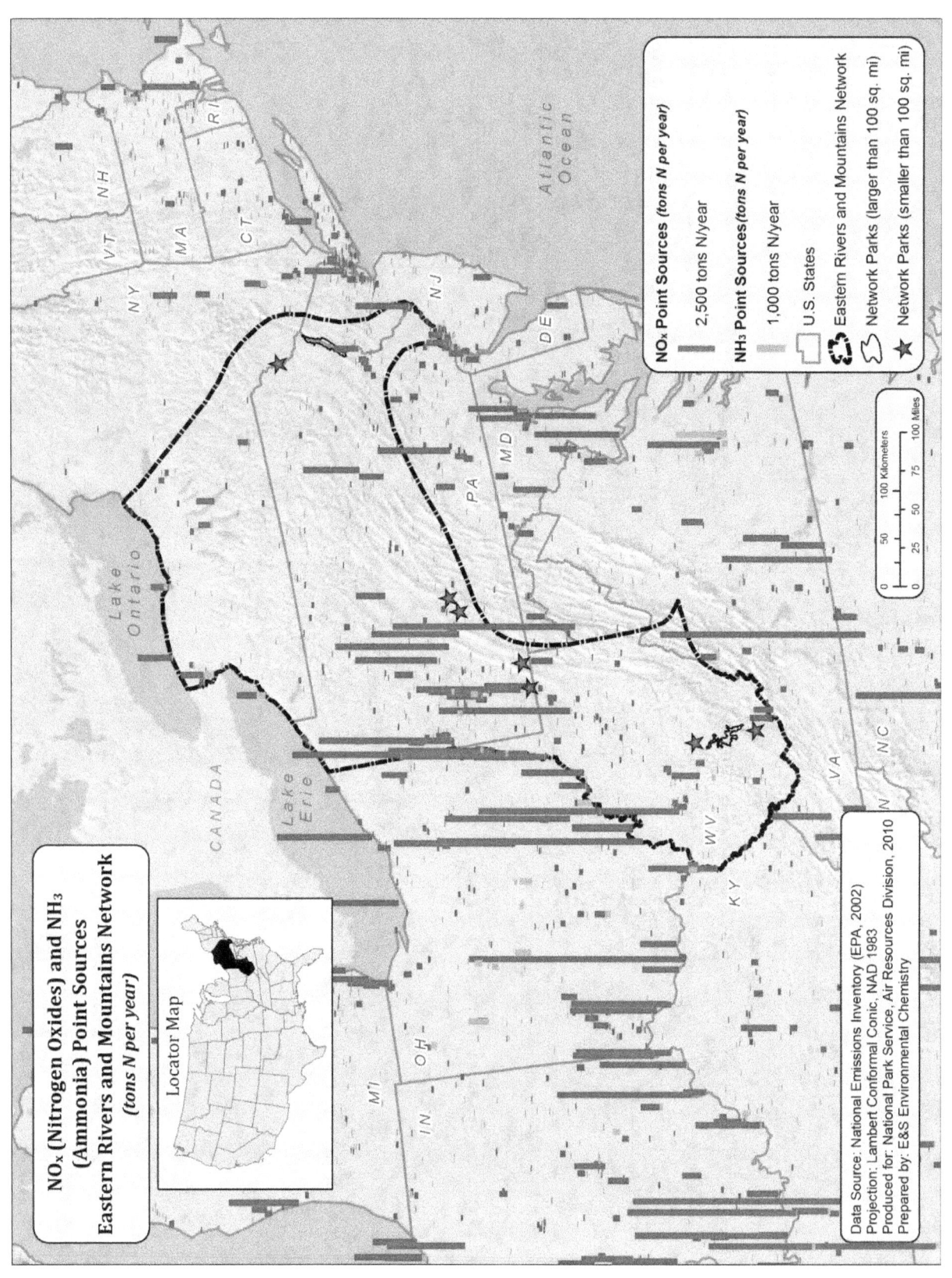

NOx (Nitrogen Oxides) and NH₃ (Ammonia) Point Sources
Eastern Rivers and Mountains Network
(tons N per year)

Locator Map

NOx Point Sources *(tons N per year)*
— 2,500 tons N/year

NH₃ Point Sources*(tons N per year)*
— 1,000 tons N/year

☐ U.S. States
⬭ Eastern Rivers and Mountains Network
♥ Network Parks (larger than 100 sq. mi)
★ Network Parks (smaller than 100 sq. mi)

Data Source: National Emissions Inventory (EPA, 2002)
Projection: Lambert Conformal Conic, NAD 1983
Produced for: National Park Service, Air Resources Division, 2010
Prepared by: E&S Environmental Chemistry

Map D

CAKN-8

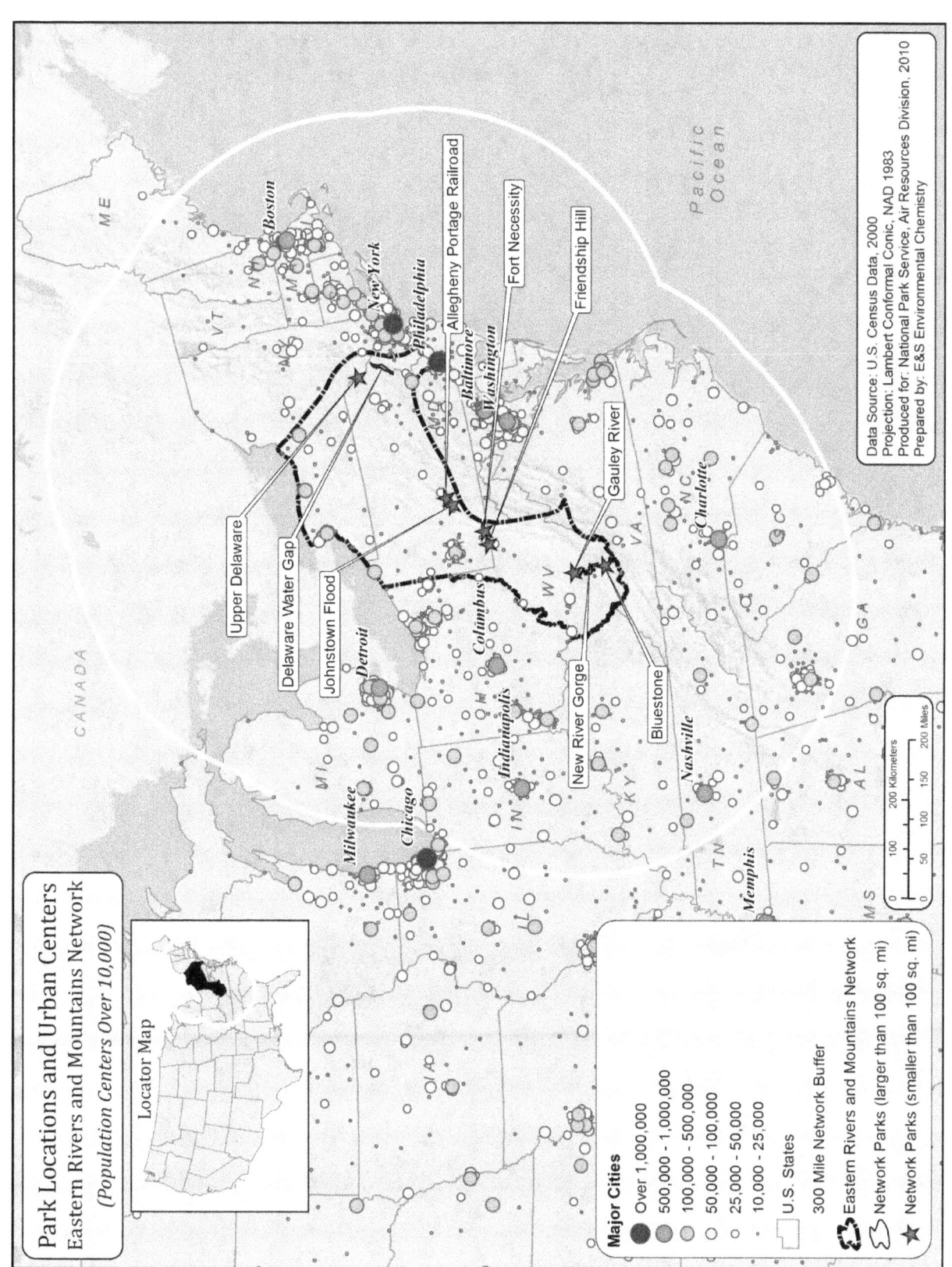

Park Locations and Urban Centers
Eastern Rivers and Mountains Network
(Population Centers Over 10,000)

Locator Map

Major Cities
- Over 1,000,000
- 500,000 - 1,000,000
- 100,000 - 500,000
- 50,000 - 100,000
- 25,000 - 50,000
- 10,000 - 25,000

U.S. States
300 Mile Network Buffer
Eastern Rivers and Mountains Network
★ Network Parks (larger than 100 sq. mi)
★ Network Parks (smaller than 100 sq. mi)

Data Source: U.S. Census Data, 2000
Projection: Lambert Conformal Conic, NAD 1983
Produced for: National Park Service, Air Resources Division, 2010
Prepared by: E&S Environmental Chemistry

Allegheny Portage Railroad
Fort Necessity
Friendship Hill
Upper Delaware
Delaware Water Gap
Johnstown Flood
Gauley River
New River Gorge
Bluestone

Boston
New York
Philadelphia
Baltimore
Washington
Detroit
Columbus
Indianapolis
Nashville
Memphis
Charlotte
Milwaukee
Chicago

CANADA
Pacific Ocean

ME
VT
NH
MA
MI
WV
VA
NC
KY
TN
IN
GA
AL
MS

Map E

CAKN-9

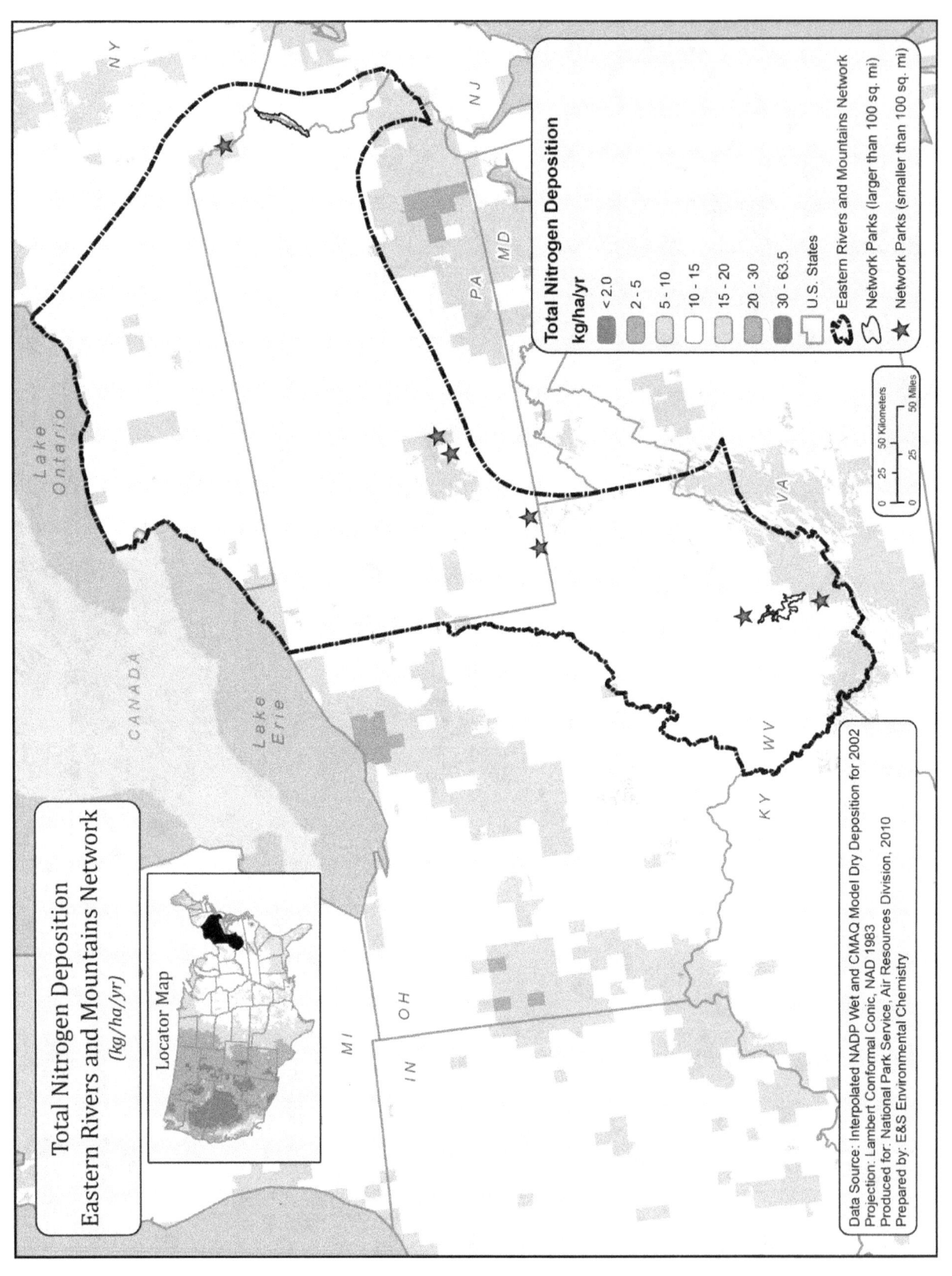

Total Nitrogen Deposition
Eastern Rivers and Mountains Network
(kg/ha/yr)

Locator Map

Total Nitrogen Deposition
kg/ha/yr
- < 2.0
- 2 - 5
- 5 - 10
- 10 - 15
- 15 - 20
- 20 - 30
- 30 - 63.5
- U.S. States
- Eastern Rivers and Mountains Network
- ★ Network Parks (larger than 100 sq. mi)
- ★ Network Parks (smaller than 100 sq. mi)

Data Source: Interpolated NADP Wet and CMAQ Model Dry Deposition for 2002
Projection: Lambert Conformal Conic, NAD 1983
Produced for: National Park Service, Air Resources Division, 2010
Prepared by: E&S Environmental Chemistry

Map F

CAKN-10

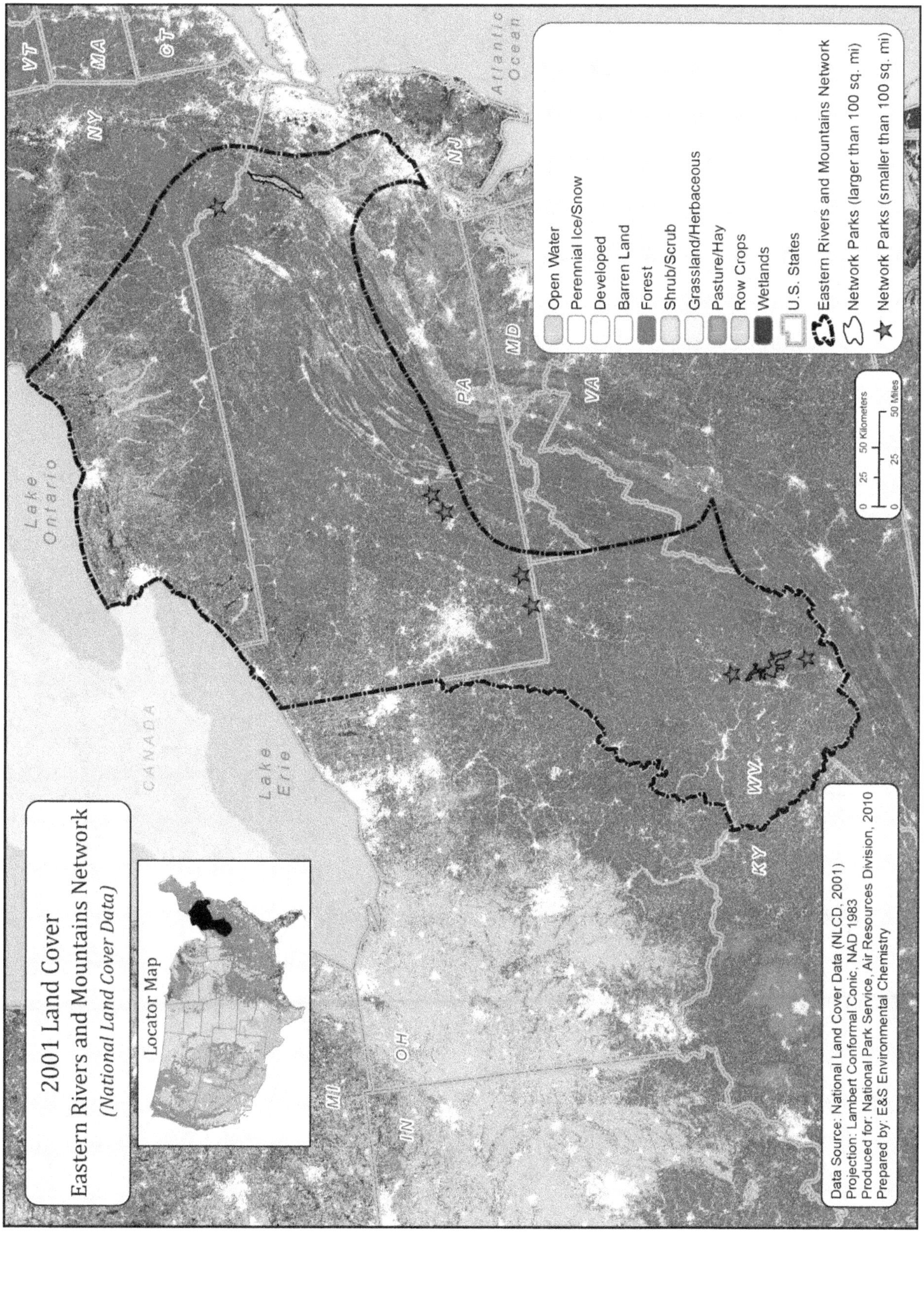

2001 Land Cover
Eastern Rivers and Mountains Network
(National Land Cover Data)
Locator Map
Lake Ontario
Lake Erie
CANADA
Atlantic Ocean
VT
MA
CT
NY
NJ
MD
PA
VA
WV
KY
OH
MI
IN
Open Water
Perennial Ice/Snow
Developed
Barren Land
Forest
Shrub/Scrub
Grassland/Herbaceous
Pasture/Hay
Row Crops
Wetlands
U.S. States
Eastern Rivers and Mountains Network
Network Parks (larger than 100 sq. mi)
Network Parks (smaller than 100 sq. mi)
0 25 50 Kilometers
0 25 50 Miles
Data Source: National Land Cover Data (NLCD, 2001)
Projection: Lambert Conformal Conic, NAD 1983
Produced for: National Park Service, Air Resources Division, 2010
Prepared by: E&S Environmental Chemistry

Map G

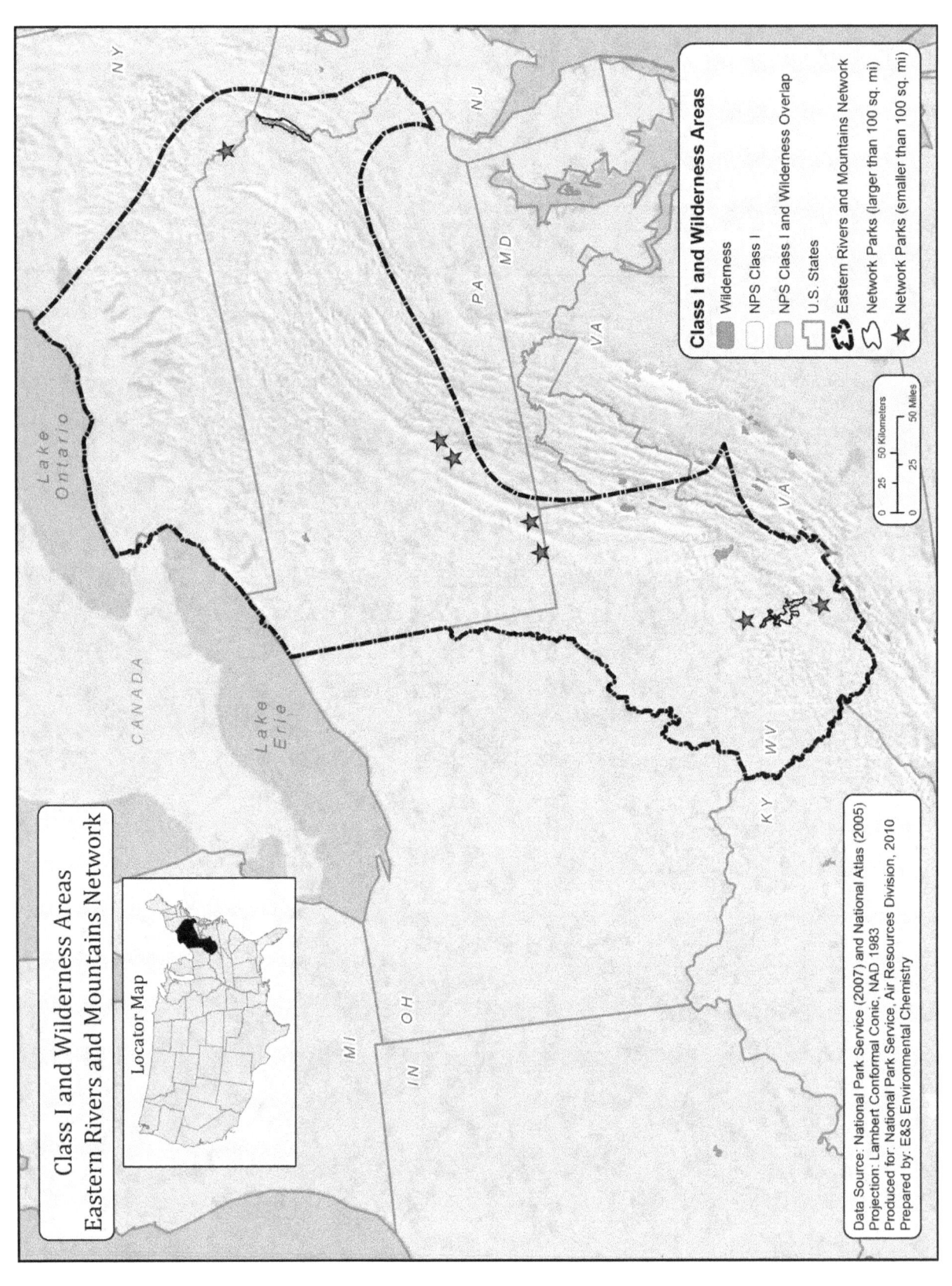

Class I and Wilderness Areas
Eastern Rivers and Mountains Network

Locator Map

Class I and Wilderness Areas

- Wilderness
- NPS Class I
- NPS Class I and Wilderness Overlap
- U.S. States
- Eastern Rivers and Mountains Network
- ★ Network Parks (larger than 100 sq. mi)
- ★ Network Parks (smaller than 100 sq. mi)

Data Source: National Park Service (2007) and National Atlas (2005)
Projection: Lambert Conformal Conic, NAD 1983
Produced for: National Park Service, Air Resources Division, 2010
Prepared by: E&S Environmental Chemistry

NY
NJ
PA
MD
VA
VA
WV
KY
OH
IN
MI
CANADA
Lake Ontario
Lake Erie

0 25 50 Kilometers
0 25 50 Miles

Map I

CAKN-12

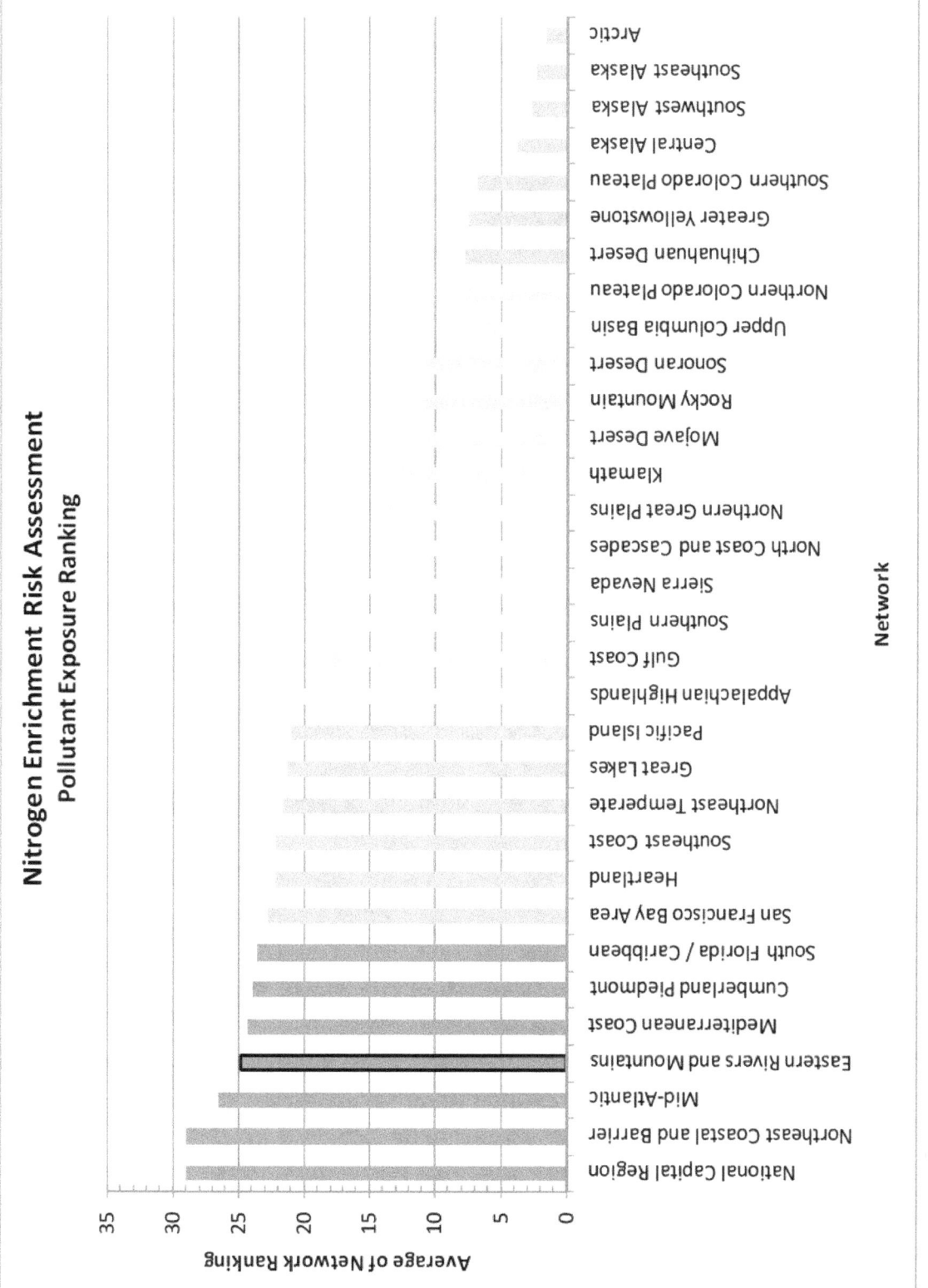

Figure A

CAKN-13

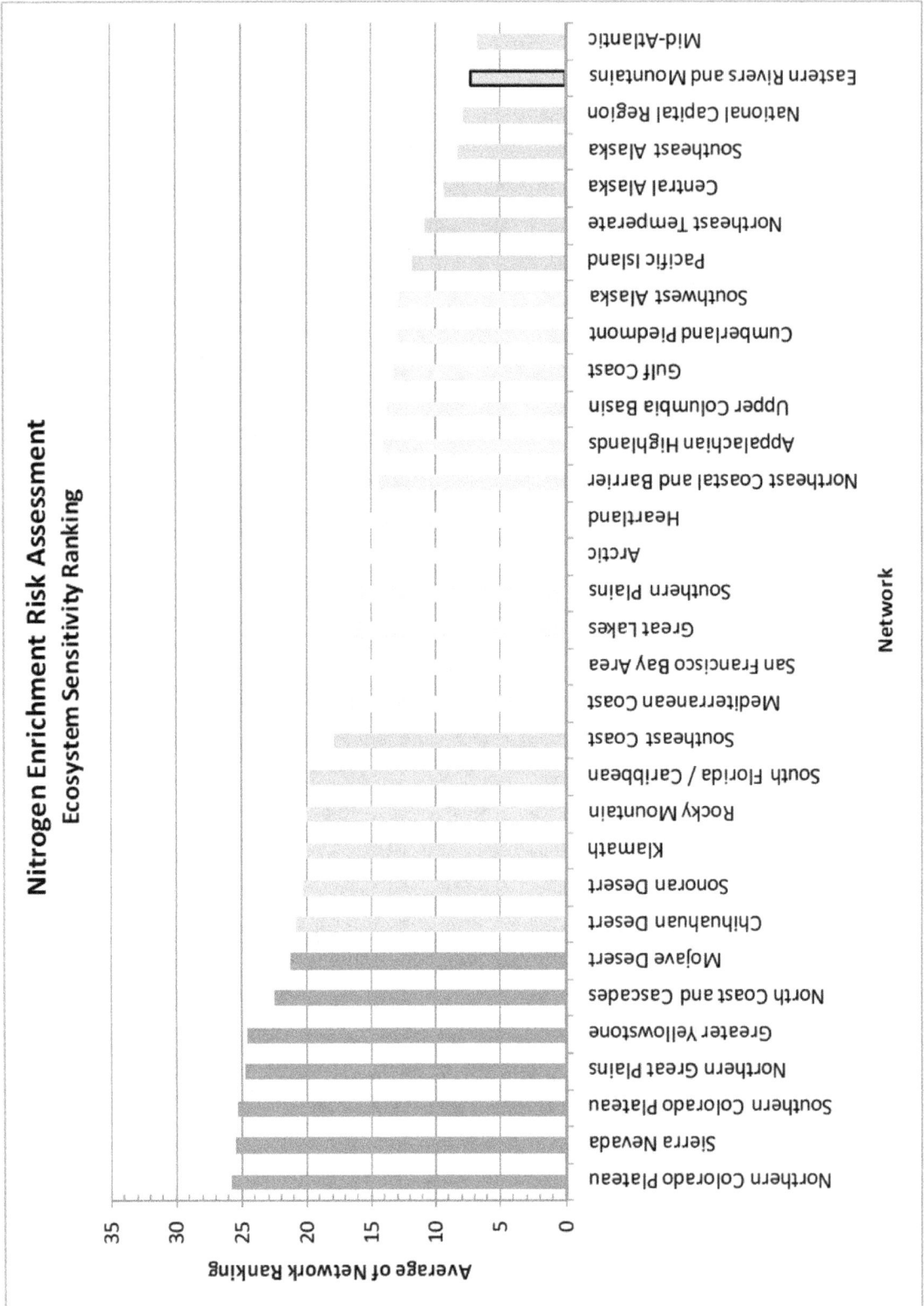

Figure B

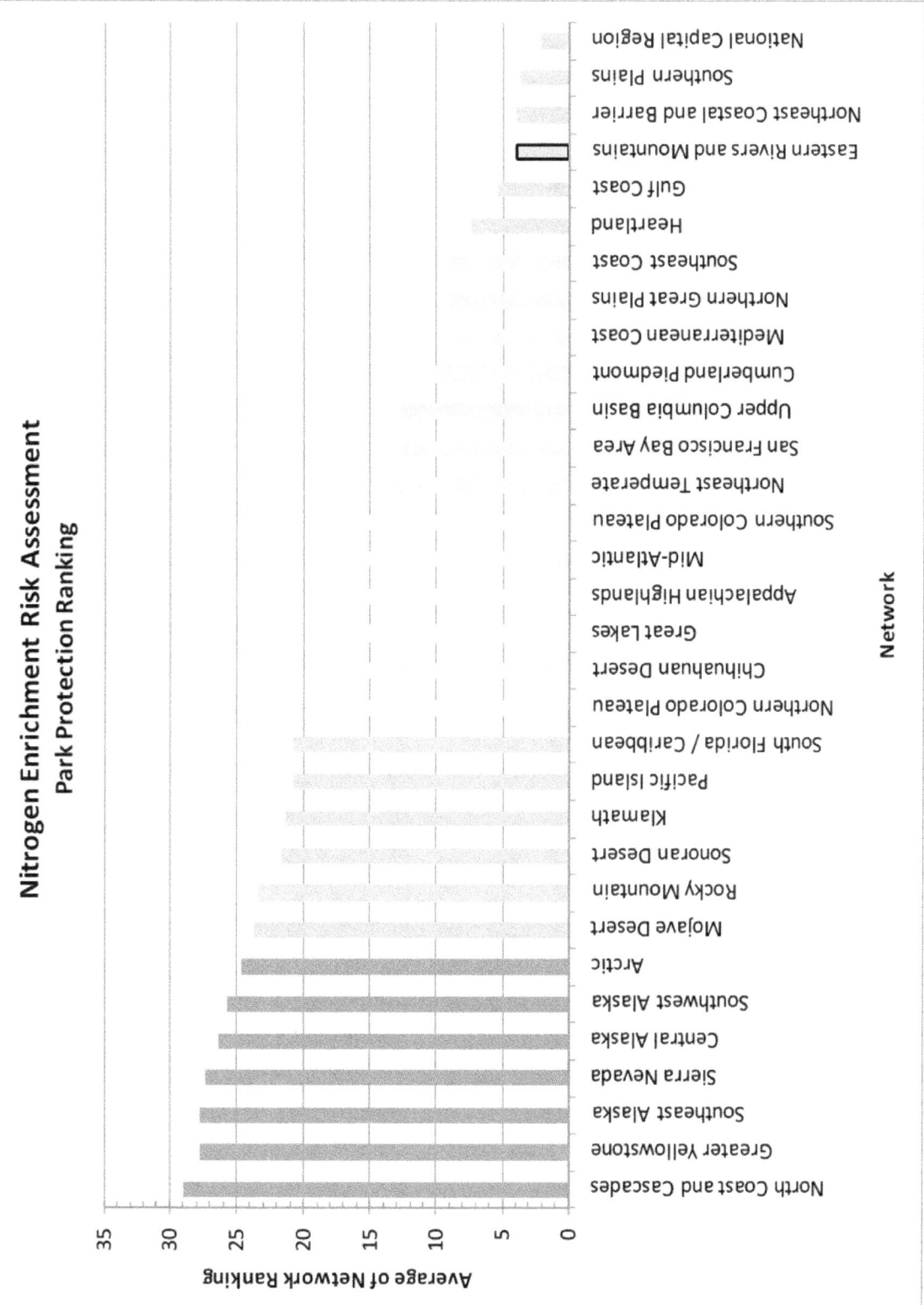

Figure C

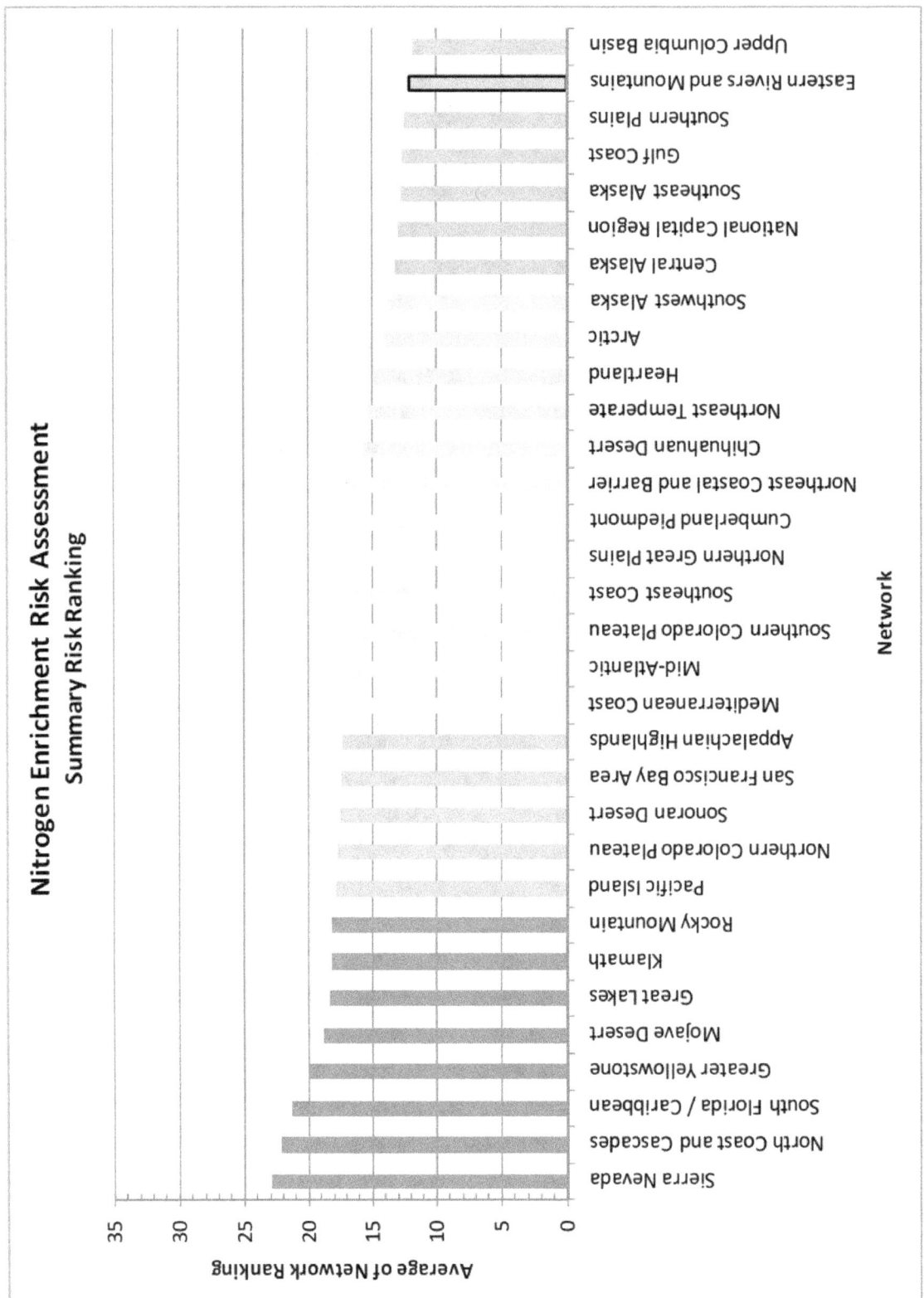

Figure D

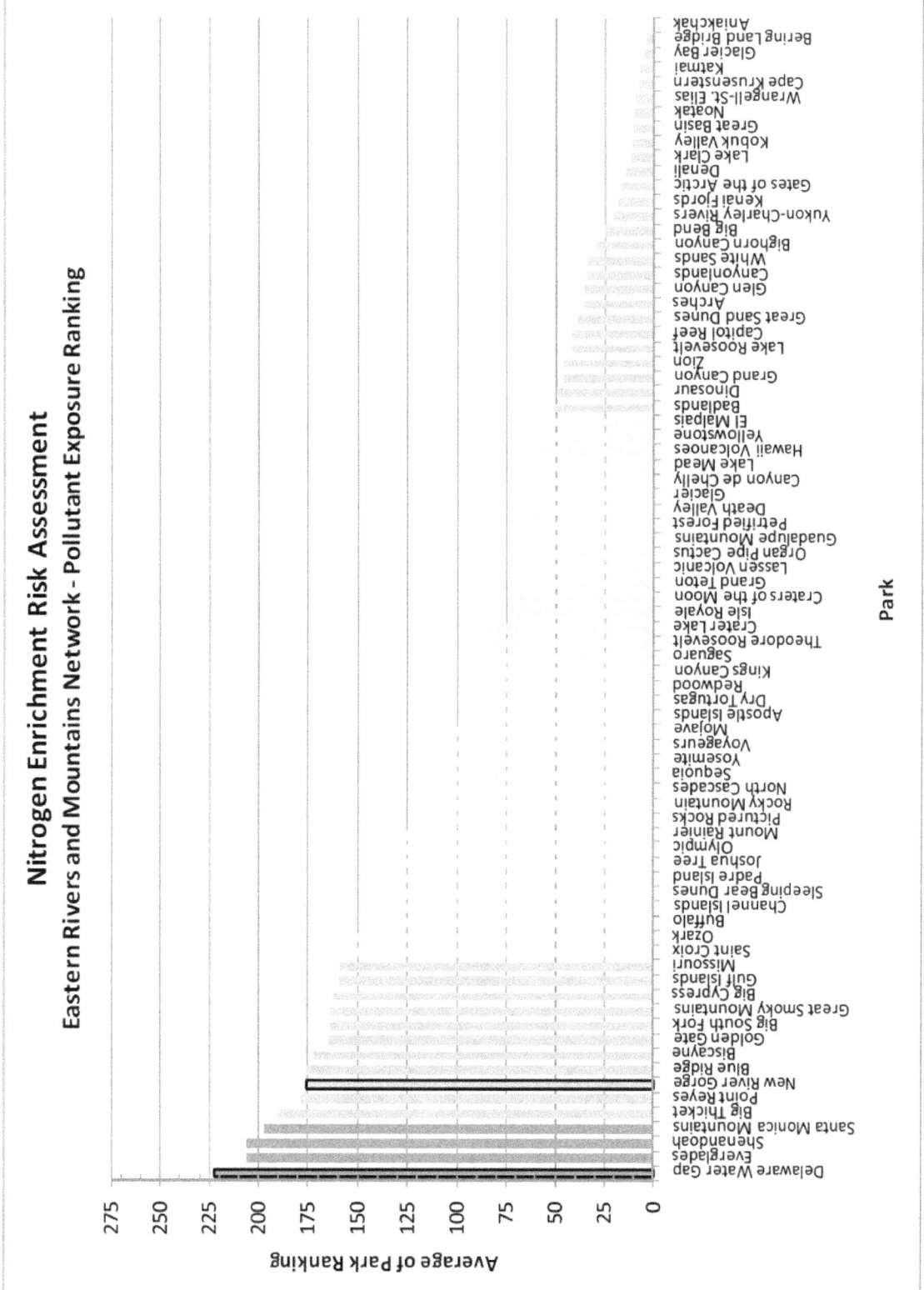

Figure E

CAKN-17

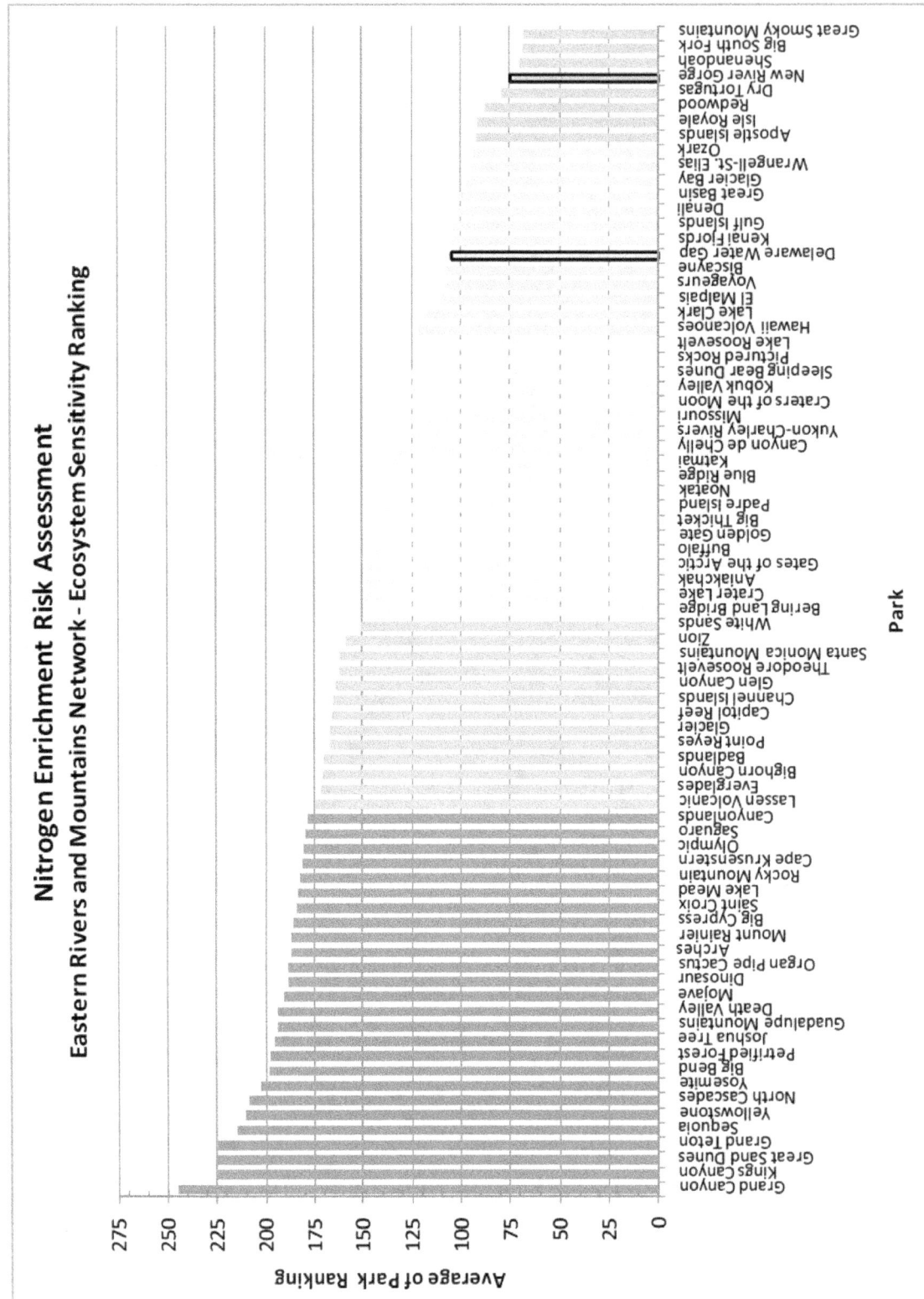

Figure F

CAKN-18

Nitrogen Enrichment Risk Assessment
Eastern Rivers and Mountains Network - Park Protection Ranking

Figure G

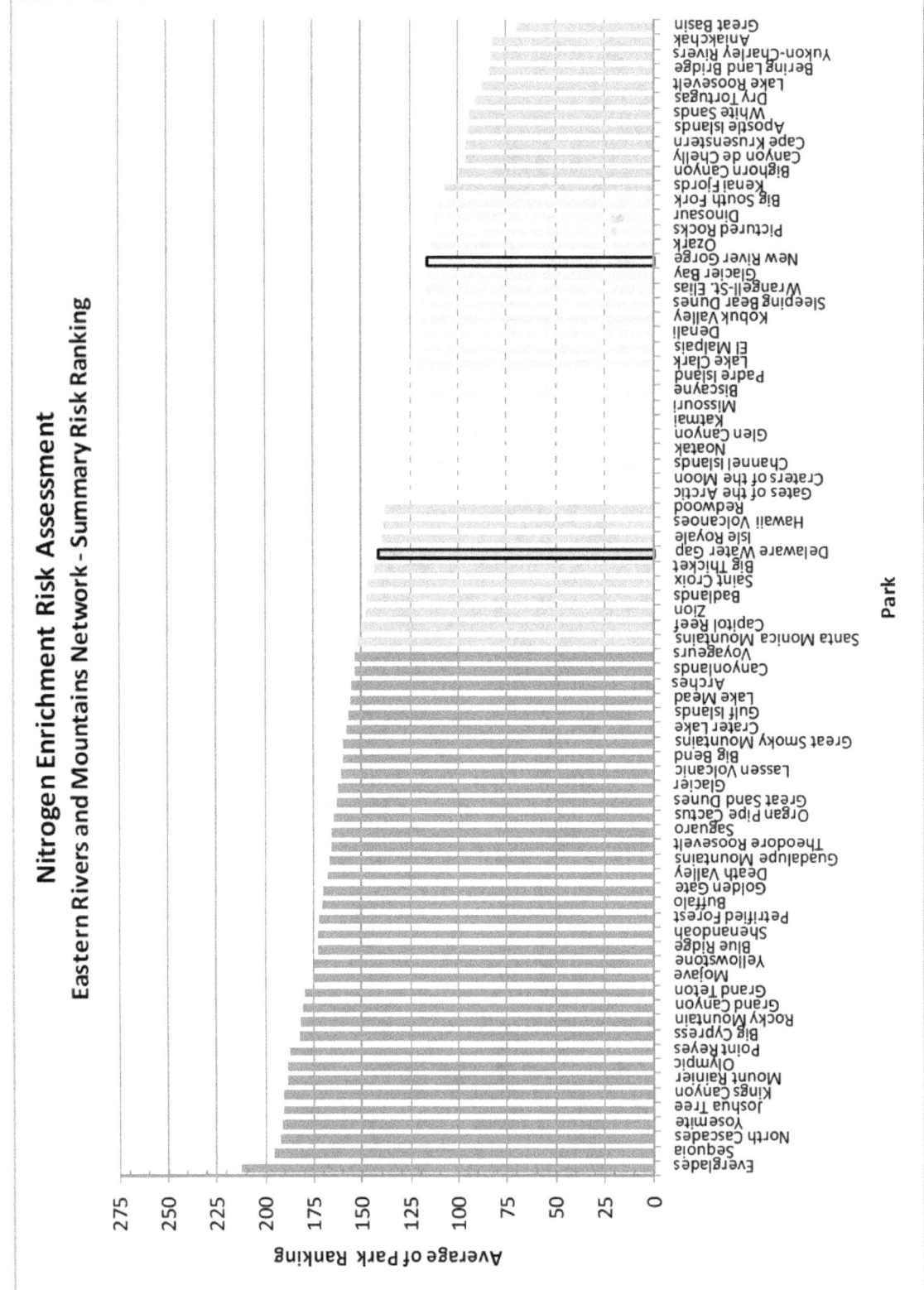

Figure H

CAKN-20

NPS 962/106647, February 2011